Contents

What you need to know about the National Tests

Preparing and practising for the English Test

English Booklet

Level 6 Booklet

What you need to know about the National Tests

KEY STAGE 2 NATIONAL TESTS: HOW THEY WORK

Pupils between the ages of 7 and 11 (Years 3–6) cover Key Stage 2 of the National Curriculum. In May of their final year of Key Stage 2 (Year 6), all pupils take written National Curriculum Statutory Tests in English, Mathematics and Science. The tests are carried out in school, under the supervision of teachers, but are marked by examiners outside the school.

The tests help to show what children have learned in these key subjects during Key Stage 2. They also help parents and teachers to know whether children are reaching the standards set out in the National Curriculum.

Each child will probably spend around five hours in total sitting the tests during one week in May. Most children will do two papers in Science and three papers in Mathematics and English.

The school sends the papers away to external examiners for marking. The school will then report the results of the tests to you by the end of July, along with the results of assessments made by teachers in the classroom, based on your child's work throughout Key Stage 2. You will also receive a summary of the results for all pupils at the school, and for pupils nationally. This will help you to compare the performance of your child with that of other children of the same age. The report from your child's school will explain to you what the results show about your child's progress, strengths, particular achievements and targets for development. It may also explain how to follow up the results with your child's teachers.

In addition, the publication of LEA primary school performance (or 'league') tables will show how your child's school has performed in the teacher assessments and tests, compared to other schools locally.

UNDERSTANDING YOUR CHILD'S LEVEL OF ACHIEVEMENT

The National Curriculum divides standards for performance in each subject into a number of levels, from one to eight. On average, children are expected to advance one level for every two years they are at school. By Year 6 (the end of Key Stage 2), your child should be at Level 4. The table on page iii shows how your child is expected to progress through the levels at ages 7, 11 and 14 (the end of Key Stages 1, 2 and 3).

Most children will take three papers for Levels 3–5 in English. The Reading and Writing Tests will each be one hour long, and the Spelling and Handwriting Test will be 15 minutes long. An Extension Paper with Level 6 questions is available for exceptionally able pupils. This paper takes one hour.

What you need to know about the National Tests

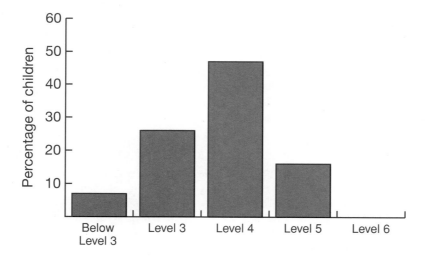

	7 years	11 years	14 years
Level 8+			
Level 8			
Level 7			
Level 6			
Level 5			
Level 4			
Level 3			
Level 2			
Level 1			

☐ Exceptional performance

■ Exceeded targets for age group

☐ Achieved targets for age group

▨ Working towards targets for age group

How your child should progress

This book concentrates on Levels 3–5, giving plenty of practice to help your child achieve the best level possible. There are also some Level 6 questions for very able pupils. Do not worry if your child cannot do the Level 6 test; remember that Level 4 is the target level for children at the end of Key Stage 2. However, you may wish to discuss some of the Level 6 questions with your child (see page v). The bar chart below shows you what percentage of pupils nationally reached each of the levels in the 1997 tests for English.

Levels achieved in English, 1997

Although the results of all reading, spelling and mathematics tests will be reported in terms of a subject level, these test scores will also be converted into an age-standardised score, to show the school how your child's score in these tests compares with that of his or her age group. In addition, you will receive your child's reading and writing levels.

Preparing and practising for the English Test

ENGLISH AT KEY STAGE 2

The questions in this book will test your child on the Key Stage 2 curriculum for English. For assessment purposes, the National Curriculum divides English into three sections, called Attainment Targets (ATs). The first AT, Speaking and Listening, is assessed only by the teacher in the classroom, not in the written tests. The other two ATs are Reading (AT2) and Writing (AT3) – including Spelling and Handwriting.

The National Curriculum describes levels of performance for each of the three English ATs. These AT levels are taken together to give an overall level for English. In addition, the test papers will assess both reading and writing and these levels will be reported to you.

USING THIS BOOK TO HELP YOUR CHILD PREPARE

This book contains four basic features:

Questions:	four test papers for Levels 3–5 in Reading, Writing, Spelling and Handwriting, and one extension paper for Level 6
Answers:	showing acceptable responses and marks
Notes to Parent:	giving advice on how to help your child avoid common mistakes and improve his or her score
Level Charts:	showing you how to interpret your child's marks to arrive at a level for each test and overall

SETTING THE TESTS AT HOME

Try setting the Reading Test first, mark it to see how your child has done and work through the answers and advice together. Then set the Writing, Spelling and Handwriting Tests on different days. Let your child carry out the tests in a place where he or she is comfortable. Your child will need a pen or pencil and a rubber may be used.

Setting the Reading Test

Detach pages 1–8 from the back of the book and fasten the pages together to make the English Booklet. The Reading Test questions are about the *Strange Tales* in this booklet.

Read through the test instructions on pages 1–2 together. You should allow your child 15 minutes to read the booklet. You might want to suggest reading "The Disastrous Dog" on pages 4–8 first, but emphasise that your child is not expected to *memorise* the readings; he or she may refer to the booklet at any time during the test.

Note the starting time in the box at the top of the test. After 45 minutes, ask your child to stop writing. If he or she has not finished, but wishes to continue working on the test, draw a line to show how much has been completed within the test time. Then let your child work to the end of the test, but check that he or she is able to cope with the questions as they become more difficult.

Preparing and practising for the English Test

Setting the Writing Test

To set the Writing Test, make sure your child has some writing paper. Read through the instructions on page 14 together. Once he or she has chosen one of the starting points for the Writing Test, you should allow your child 15 minutes to plan his or her writing. Then note the starting time on the top of the first sheet of writing paper. After 45 minutes, ask your child to stop writing.

Setting the Spelling and Handwriting Tests

The Spelling Test requires you to detach page 39 and read out a story to your child. Your child will be asked to fill in the missing words on his or her version of the story on pages 18–19. The test should take about 10 minutes. The Handwriting Test asks your child to copy out a passage on page 20 in his or her best joined-up handwriting. The Handwriting Test should take 5 minutes.

Setting the Level 6 Test

The Level 6 Test is an Extension Paper, designed to assess the Reading and Writing of exceptionally able children. Your child should only attempt to take the Level 6 Test if the results of the Levels 3–5 Tests suggest that he or she is working at the higher end of Level 5 in *both* the Reading and Writing Tests. If you decide that the test is too difficult for your child, you may still make use of the material by working through the test orally. Detach pages 9–18 from the back of the book and fasten the pages together to make the Level 6 Booklet. Read the story "Teeth" and the article on Anita Roddick in the booklet and discuss how these passages are written. This could be an opportunity to extend your child's awareness of character, plot and the way authors use words and language. You could also use the questions in this test as starting points for discussing a particular aspect of the story or article.

MARKING THE QUESTIONS

When your child has completed a test, turn to the Answers section at the back of the book. Work through the answers with your child, using the Notes to Parent to help give advice, correct mistakes and explain problems. If your child required extra time to complete a test, go through all the questions with your child, but do not include the marks for the "extra" questions in the total scores.

You can help a child who tends to work slowly to use time more effectively:

- identify specific amounts of time needed to complete sections of a test, e.g. 15 minutes in the Writing Test to write an introduction;

- if the child is struggling with a question, ask him or her to read it through aloud, then ask if the child knows what the question means – this often helps clarify whether or not the child can respond to the question;

- encourage your child to move on to the next question if he or she gets really stuck;

- identify areas of the Reading Test where the questions are easier – usually, the beginning of each section, e.g. pages 3 and 8.

Preparing and practising for the English Test

Using the recommended answers, award your child the appropriate mark or marks for each question. In the margin of each test page, there are small boxes divided in half. The marks available for each question are at the bottom; write your child's score in the top half of the box.

Enter the total number of marks for each section on the Marking Grid on page 48. This will enable you to calculate your child's Reading, Writing and English test level. Then add them up to find the total for the test. Look at the charts on page 47 to determine your child's level for each test, as well as an overall level.

FINALLY, AS THE TESTS DRAW NEAR

In the days before the tests, make sure your child is as relaxed and confident as possible. You can help by:

- ensuring your child knows what test papers he or she will be doing;

- working through practice questions, and discussing which answers are right and why.

Although the National Tests are important, your child's achievement throughout the school year is equally important. Encourage your child to do his or her best without putting him or her under too much pressure. Many children find that they enjoy doing tests, but it is natural that some may be nervous. Look out for signs of anxiety, such as changes in eating or sleeping habits, and reassure your child if he or she is worried about these tests.

Instructions

Carefully detach pages 1–8 from the back of this book. Fasten the pages together to make your own English Booklet. The questions in this reading test are about the *Strange Tales* in your booklet. This test is divided into two main parts: 'Amazing U.F.O.s' (about a poem and an informative passage about U.F.O.s) and a story called *The Disastrous Dog*.

Your parent will give you 15 minutes to read your booklet before you begin the test. You may wish to start reading *The Disastrous Dog* on pages 4–8 first. Don't worry if you do not finish reading the whole section. You may look at the booklet as often as you wish during the test.

The written part of this test should take about 45 minutes.

Read all the words in the test carefully.

Some questions will give you a choice of answers. You will be asked to ring the right answer, like this:

The title of the story about the dog is

The Animal   The Amazing   (The Disastrous   The Dog that
Sanctuary   Dog   Dog)   could Talk   .

Some questions only require a word or phrase as an answer and have a short space or line, for example:

Write down which day comes after Monday.

....

Reading Test

Some questions ask for an answer which is a bit longer. To answer these questions, you will be given two or three lines, for example:

Explain what you enjoy doing at weekends.

....

....

Some questions towards the end of the test require a long answer. These questions often ask you to give reasons for your answer, and to use the text in the English booklet to help you explain why you have a particular opinion. These questions will have a box where you should write your answer, for example:

Do you think that the *Strange Tales* in the English booklet are interesting?

Yes ☐   No ☐

By referring to the booklet, explain your answer.

....

....

....

Write your answer on the blank line or lines, or in the box provided. Look for the ▭▷ to show you where to write your answer.

After finishing a page, turn over to a new page without waiting to be told. If a question is too hard, you should move on to the next question.

GOOD LUCK!

Start		Finish	

Strange Tales: Amazing U.F.O.s

These questions are about the poem "U.F.O." on page 1 of your English Booklet.

1

> **This poem is about a series of events. Describe in your own words TWO events that take place.**

✏ 1 ....

2 ....

1
Q1

2

> **The poet talks about what she sees and hears. Write down TWO things that the poet sees and TWO things that she hears.**

✏ **a sees**   1 .... 2 ....

b hears   1 .... 2 ....

2
Q2

3

> **Write down the word from the poem that rhymes with *humming*.**

✏ ....

1
Q3

Letts

4

> Write down another TWO words that rhyme in this poem.

.... rhymes with ....

5

> Describe how rhyme is used in this poem.

....

These questions are about "Target Earth" on page 2 of your English Booklet.

6

> What was special about 1952?

....

....

7

> At what TWO times of the year are you most likely to see a U.F.O.?

1 .... 2 ....

8 The passage says: *Once the idea of U.F.O.s has been planted in people's minds they are more likely to start "meeting Martians".*

> **Why do you think this happens?**

1
Q8

These questions are about "The Washington Invasion" on page 2 of your English Booklet.

9

> **What did people see in Washington on 19th July 1952?**

1
Q9

Reading Test

10 a

How could people tell that the lights seen on 26th July were not aeroplanes?

....

....

1
Q10a

b

What were the pilots trying to do?

....

....

1
Q10b

These questions are about "The Flying Cross" on page 3 of your English booklet.

11

On 24th October 1967 two policemen saw a "flying cross". What did they see?

....

....

1
Q11

12

What happened when the policemen chased the flying cross?

....

....

1
Q12

13 Two possible explanations were given for the flying cross.

a

> **What was the first explanation?**

✏ ....

....

Q13a

b

> **What is wrong with this explanation?**

✏ ....

....

Q13b

c

> **What was the second explanation?**

✏ ....

....

Q13c

d

> **What words or phrases show that the writer does not believe this explanation?**

✏ ....

....

....

Q13d

Strange Tales: The Disastrous Dog

These questions are about the story "The Disastrous Dog" on pages 4–8 of your English Booklet.

Draw a ring around the word or group of words that best completes these sentences.

1   To get a dog, Paul and his family went to

| a pet shop | a vet's surgery | an Animal Sanctuary | a hospital for sick animals |

.

2   Mr and Mrs Roper took the dog because he

| put on an act | was able to speak | looked sad and lonely | was very old |

.

3   The first time the dog was taken for a walk he

| barked loudly | started limping | ran excitedly | kept rolling over |

.

4   When Mr Roper took him for a five-mile walk the dog

| did clever tricks | got even fatter | rolled in mud | wanted to walk further |

.

5   When Mr Roper decided not to keep the dog, Paul

| felt sad | took him back | felt relieved | took care of him |

.

These questions are about what happened in the story.

6

> **The dog thought Paul's home would be a nice place to live. Why?**

....

....

....

2
Q6

7

> **Why did Mr and Mrs Roper decide to choose the dog as a pet?**

....

....

2
Q7

8 The dog wanted his basket moved from the cloakroom to the kitchen.

a

> **Why did he want to sleep in the kitchen?**

....

1
Q8a

b

> **What did he *do* to persuade Mrs Roper to move his basket?**

....

1
Q8b

9 People called at the house each day.

a

> **How did the dog behave to the postman on the first day?**

1
Q9a

....

b

> **How did the dog behave to the window-cleaner on the fifth day?**

1
Q9b

....

10

> **Why did Mr Roper finally decide to send the dog back to the Animal Sanctuary?**

1
Q10

....

....

These questions are about the characters in the story.

11

> **The dog first spoke to Paul at the Animal Sanctuary. How did Paul feel about the dog after he spoke?**

1
Q11

....

12

> **Mrs Roper is soft-hearted. Write down THREE things she says or does that show that she is soft-hearted.**

1 ....

2 ....

3 ....

Q12

13

> **Mrs Roper's attitude towards the dog changed during the story. Complete these sentences to show how her attitude changed.**

a At first she thought ....

b When the dog seemed ill she felt ....

c When he got mud on the carpet she was ....

Q13

These questions ask about how the story is written.

14

> **The dog often speaks in a rather unpleasant way. Find THREE words or phrases that the author uses to describe the unpleasant way the dog speaks to Paul.**

1 ....

2 ....

3 ....

Q14

15 The author writes: *His attacks on the postman were more and more unconvincing.*

> **What does she mean by this?**

....

....

1
Q15

These questions ask you for your opinion.

16

> **Why do you think that the dog talked to Paul and not to Mr and Mrs Roper?**

....

....

....

....

3
Q16

17 Would you have liked to have this dog as a pet?

Yes ☐ No ☐

Why do you think this? Explain the reasons for your answer.

....
....
....

2
Q17

18 Did you enjoy reading this story?

Yes ☐ No ☐

Explain the reasons for your answer.

....
....
....
....

3
Q18

Instructions

Ask your parent to read the notes on page v before you begin this writing test. Then read the instructions below.

On pages 15–17 there are five starting points for the writing test. Read through all the starting points with your parent. Choose **one** starting point to work on for the test.

Write down the number and title of the starting point you have chosen:

Starting point number ....

Title ....

Planning

Your parent will give you one or two sheets of paper for you to note ideas about what you are going to write.

If you are planning to write story **1, 2 or 3**, think about:
- how to start your story in an interesting way;
- getting into the story quickly;
- making sure that the order of events is clear;
- including only a small number of characters;
- planning a good ending.

If you are planning to write letter **4 or 5**, try to think about:
- what you are writing and why;
- organising your ideas so that they make sense to the reader;
- giving some details and explanations to make the writing interesting;
- planning a good ending.

You will have 15 minutes to plan your writing. Remember that *planning* should help you to get your ideas for your writing in order. The plan is *not* marked. Try to write your ideas quickly; you do not have to use full sentences and your spelling and handwriting are not so important.

The test

Next, your parent will give you some more paper. Write your name and the title of your writing at the top of the first sheet.

You will have 45 minutes to do your writing. GOOD LUCK!

1 Oh, No!

> *It was when we got home that the trouble began . . .*
> **Write a short story using this idea to help you.**

You should think about:

- the people in the story;
- what the "trouble" was;
- how it all started;
- what happened.

2 A New Friend

> **Write a short story about somebody who makes a new friend. (One of the people in the story could be you.)**

You should think about:

- the people in the story;
- how they meet;
- how they become friends.

3   # Out of the Dark

> **Write a short story with the title "Out of the Dark".**

You should think about:

- where the events take place;

- who or what comes *out of
  the dark*;

- the other people in the story;

- what happens.

4   # Please Look After this Bear!

Many people do not take proper care of their pets. You could
call them disastrous owners!

> **Write a letter to somebody who is about to buy a pet.
> Explain what that person should do in order to be a
> responsible owner.**

You should think about:

- what sort of pet the person
  is buying;

- what the pet will need
  (bedding, cage, etc.);

- how to care for the pet (e.g.
  food, exercise, health);

- other important information.

5   ## Strange but True

Read this passage from "The Flying Cross":

Police constables Roger Willey and Clifford Waycott were on routine night duty in their patrol car when they suddenly saw bright lights in the shape of a large cross pulsating in the sky ahead of them. As the patrol car drove towards it, the cross moved silently away. The policemen chased through the narrow lanes after it, but the cross always managed to accelerate away from them. Eventually it moved off across the fields and the policemen gave up.

> **Write a letter to one of the policemen who saw the flying cross.**

The letter can come from:

- somebody who also saw the lights and believes in U.F.O.s;

or

- somebody who does not believe in U.F.O.s and thinks there is another explanation.

35
Writing
Test

Spelling Test

Instructions

This Spelling Test will take about 10 minutes.

Your parent will read the story called "U.F.O.s??" on page 39 out loud twice. You will follow along with your version of the story below, which has some words missing.

As your parent reads the story out loud for the first time, follow along with your version, but do not write anything. Then your parent will read the story for the second time.

When you come to a gap, wait for your parent to tell you the word. Write the missing word on the line. If you are not sure how to spell the word, just try to write the letters you think are correct.

U.F.O.s??

Jenny and her brother Paul had heard stories about U.F.O.s landing in the field next to their house. During the summer holidays they set their alarm clocks so that they could wake up in the middle of the night…

One night, as they .... out of the window everything was .... but something seemed .... The .... was quite strange: it felt as though something .... happen at any ....

6

The children listened carefully, ... on any new sound. At last they .... a humming sound which seemed to be coming .... Paul gave a loud .... and the earth .... – or that is how it seemed! A second later, a .... light appeared and a huge spaceship seemed to .... to the ground.

The children .... closer to the window and watched as the door of the spaceship opened. Through the door came the .... people they had ever seen. The .... were wearing the most .... uniforms, covered in ....

Paul gave a loud snore and then .... Jenny was .... across her bed in a deep sleep. Did a U.F.O. land last night or was it all a dream?

Handwriting Test

Instructions

This short passage continues the story from the spelling test.

Write out the passage below very neatly in your own handwriting. Remember to join your letters if you can.

You have 5 minutes to do this test.

Take-off!

"All aboard!" shouted the spaceship captain. Once the crew were at their stations, they prepared for take-off very quickly. "Three, two, one, zero," the captain counted. Slowly, the spacecraft rose from the ground and drifted up into the sky. It slipped away into the darkness just as the children were waking up.

Write the passage on these lines.

The Level 6 Test is very challenging. Before you continue, make sure your parent has read the notes on page v about this test.

Level 6 Test

Instructions

Before you start, think about how you are going to use your time during the test. You will have 60 minutes to do this test. This includes the time you have to read pages 9–18 of the Level 6 Booklet.

The questions in the test are based on the story "Teeth" on pages 9–14 and the article about Anita Roddick on pages 15–18 of the booklet.

You should try to answer each question as fully as you can.

When a question asks you to explain your reasons, or to use examples from the story or passage, you should remember to do this.

Try to have a watch or clock nearby so that you can check that you are not spending too much time on one question or section of the test.

You should allow at least 25 minutes to work on the last question, which asks you to do some writing.

Before you start the last question, you should spend about 5 minutes planning your writing.

Ask your parent for some writing paper for the last question.

GOOD LUCK!

Start		Finish	

Questions about the story "Teeth"　　　Questions 1–4

1　　On page 9, the narrator says: *You need a double-page spread to take in Eric these days*.

What does he mean by this?

....

....

....

2　　The narrator uses the phrase *as far as it goes* twice as a comment on Eric's story in the newspaper.

What effect does the repetition of this phrase have?

....

....

....

3

What does the narrator think of people wanting to buy Victorian baths with claw feet?

....

....

4 There are many ways in which the author makes the story especially entertaining.

> **Using examples from the story, write about the amusing ideas and language she uses.**

....

....

....

Questions about Anita Roddick   Questions 5–8

5

> **What irritated Anita Roddick so much that she decided to open her own business?**

....

....

....

6   Anita Roddick used unusual ways to promote her products.

a

What did she do that was so unusual?

....

....

....

....

b

Why did people seem to like what she was doing?

....

....

....

7   Anita Roddick travels for five months every year – but she is not on holiday.

Why does she travel?

....

....

8

Why does Anita Roddick think that it is better to *share* than to give or receive?

___

Questions about the story "Teeth" and Anita Roddick

Questions 9–11

9   Eric Donnelly and Anita Roddick are both successful but have used different approaches to business.

Whose approach do you prefer? Explain your reasons.

___

10   Eric Donnelly and Anita Roddick both say they are interested in world peace.

> **What other interests do they have that are similar?**

....

....

11   You are asked to write an article for your local newspaper on an unusual and successful business person. As Eric Donnelly and Anita Roddick are both visiting your town, you decide to write an article about one of them. You must use the passages you have read on either Eric or Anita as background information for your article.

In planning this writing, you should think about:

- how Eric or Anita has succeeded;

- what difficulties he or she may have had in achieving success;

- Eric's or Anita's interests;

- how you will make the article interesting to read.

> **Write the article on separate paper.**

Answers

HOW TO MARK THE READING TEST

Re-read the *Strange Tales* English Booklet (pages 1–8) before marking your child's answers to the Reading Test. This will help to clarify the marking scheme and will also help you to judge whether the content of an answer is correct. Different children have different ways of wording a correct answer; you need to judge whether your child had "the right idea".

Amazing U.F.O.s | Pages 3–7

1
- humming noise/roaring noise
- bright lights/shining lights in the sky
- U.F.O./spaceship comes
- the spaceship lands
- door of spaceship opens
- aliens/crew walk through the door

*Any two events: 1 mark for **both** events*   *1 mark*

2 a sees: the bright light, the U.F.O., the door, the crew
Any two answers   *1 mark*
b hears: the humming *and* roar of the U.F.O.
Both answers required   *1 mark*

3 coming   *1 mark*

4 Accept any **one** of the following pairs:
- light and bright
- air and there
- roar and door
- crew and through   *1 mark*

5 Accept answers that indicate "pairs of lines rhyme" or "words at the end of every two lines rhyme".   *1 mark*

> ### Note to parent
> These questions ask your child to identify the main ideas of the poem and provide evidence from the text of the poem to support his or her ideas. Your child also has to recognise rhyming language and the form that has been used in writing the poem.

6 there were many sightings of U.F.O.s   *1 mark*

7 spring
summer (or July)
Both needed for the mark   *1 mark*

8 Accept any reasonable answer that connects seeing U.F.O.s with meeting Martians, e.g. "Once people believe that U.F.O.s are landing, they imagine that Martians are on board the spacecraft."   *1 mark*

9 they saw five strange lights which moved for hours over the White House
or strange lights in the sky over Washington   *1 mark*

10 a they moved too fast to be aircraft   *1 mark*
b they were looking for the lights *or* they were trying to investigate the lights   *1 mark*

11 a bright light in the sky in the shape of a cross   *1 mark*

12 it always accelerated away from them *or* moved silently away — *1 mark*

13 **a** that they had seen a tanker plane — *1 mark*
b the refuelling of the planes had taken place much earlier — *1 mark*
c the policemen had chased the planet Venus — *1 mark*
d the writer says that:
"This seems unlikely…" — *1 mark*
"the flying cross mystery has never been solved" — *1 mark*

Amazing U.F.O.s Total: 19 marks

Note to parent

In the information writing on U.F.O.s, your child was asked to locate information, to use information and to identify sentences and phrases that show what the writer's views are.

The Disastrous Dog · *Pages 8–13*

1 an Animal Sanctuary — *1 mark*

2 put on an act — *1 mark*

3 started limping — *1 mark*

4 rolled in mud — *1 mark*

5 felt relieved — *1 mark*

6 because Paul's home:
- was a house
- had central heating
- was in the country
- had a garden
Up to two reasons: 1 mark; more than two reasons: 2 marks — *2 marks*

7 Accept answers that indicate they thought:
- the dog would be very obedient
- the dog was sweet
- the dog would make a good guard dog
One reason: 1 mark, two or more reasons: 2 marks — *2 marks*

8 **a** the boiler was in the kitchen and it would be warm/cosy — *1 mark*
b he pretended to be ill — *1 mark*

9 **a** he barked at him *or* tried to frighten him — *1 mark*
b he stayed asleep — *1 mark*

10 The dog had ignored the television men who came when everyone was out — *1 mark*

Note to parent

The first ten questions ask your child to identify the main events of the story. If your child had difficulty with these, read through the story together, helping your child to clarify the events and understand what happened.

11 Credit any answer which indicates that Paul was fascinated or intrigued. *1 mark*

12 Accept the following examples:
- when she first saw the dog, she said "Oh, isn't he sweet!"
- she moved his basket to a warmer place when she thought the dog was ill
- she thought he was an old dog and they should not expect too much of him
- she gave the dog three meals a day
- when he didn't bark at the television men, she suggested that the dog knew the difference between television repair men and burglars

Up to two examples: 1 mark; more than two examples: 2 marks *2 marks*

13 **a** he was sweet *1 mark*
     b sympathetic *or* sorry for him *1 mark*
     c annoyed *or* fed up *or* not pleased *1 mark*

Note to parent

Questions 11–13 about the characters in the story are more difficult. Your child is asked to glean information about their characteristics from what they said and how they acted. If your child had difficulty with these questions, you should re-read the story together, focusing on how different characters behaved. Help your child to "say" any answers they got wrong before trying to correct them in writing.

14
- bossy
- interrupted
- spluttered contemptuously
- snapped
- snarled
- sullenly

Up to two examples: 1 mark; more than two examples: 2 marks *2 marks*

15 Credit answers that indicate that the dog's attacks on the postman became less fierce and it was obvious that he was not going to harm him. *1 mark*

16 Accept any reasonable response(s) that have an explanation. E.g. it would not be sufficient to write that "The dog said that only children could hear him". An acceptable response would be "Although the dog said that only children could hear him, I think he didn't speak to them because they would have thought it worrying to have a pet that could speak".

Up to three reasons explained: 1 mark each *3 marks*

17 Accept reasons which explain the Yes/No response. E.g. it is not sufficient to say "I think it would be fun" but "I think it would be fun to have a dog that talked" would be acceptable.

Up to two reasons: 1 mark; more than two reasons: 2 marks *2 marks*

18 Award **1** mark for an answer which simply shows a preference, e.g.:
- it was great
- it was stupid
- it was funny

Award **2** marks for an answer which is referenced to the text or expresses a clear opinion, e.g.:
- I think that the dog was sarcastic and I thought that was funny.
- I like magical stories which keep you guessing about what will happen next.
- I was upset when the boy was unhappy with the dog.
- I didn't like the story because the dog made everyone disappointed.

Award **3** marks for an answer which shows that your child has understood the content and themes of the story, e.g.:
- I knew what was going to happen from the start as the dog was so bossy. I don't think that it was very interesting but it could have been better if it was longer with more action in it.
- I loved this story. All children want a dog but I wouldn't have wanted one like Mick. I was glad that Mick was sent back at the end, he deserved it.
- I felt sorry for Paul as the dog became an enemy and not a friend. I feel sorry for whoever gets Mick in the future.

3 marks

The Disastrous Dog Total: 31 marks

Note to parent

The last five questions are challenging. To answer these, your child needs to refer to the text and use this information to explain his or her reasons and responses. Children often "know" the answer but do not have the vocabulary to explain what they mean. Again, it should help if your child can "say" an answer before trying to write it.

Enter the total marks scored on each section of the Reading Test on the Marking Grid on page 48. Then turn to page 47 to determine your child's level for Reading.

HOW TO MARK THE WRITING TEST

Before you mark your child's writing, read it through at least twice so that you become familiar with it. There are two marking keys: use the key on pages 32–3 if your child wrote a story; use the key on pages 34–5 if your child wrote a letter. The key will ask you questions about how your child's writing is written and organised, what style of writing is used and how punctuation is used.

After you have read the instructions below on how to use the marking key, read the example on pages 36–8 to see how Anna's story was marked using the key for stories.

Begin with the "Just below Level 3" questions for "How is the story/letter written and organised?". Tick the "yes" or "no" box for each question at this level. Then go on to consider the questions for each level in this section in turn. You may find that you do not answer "yes" to all the questions for one level. When this happens, look at how you answered the questions for the level below and the level above – which level has the most "yes" answers? Decide which level best describes how your child's writing is written and organised. Enter the number of marks for that level on the Marking Grid on page 48.

Next, answer the questions for "What style of writing is used?" in the same way. These questions ask you to consider the vocabulary your child has used and how sentences have been constructed. Decide which level best describes your child's writing style and enter the number of marks for that level on the Marking Grid on page 48.

Do the same for "How is punctuation used?". These questions ask you to evaluate your child's use of capital letters, full stops, question marks, etc. Decide on the level that best describes your child's punctuation and enter the number of marks for that level on the Marking Grid on page 48.

The marks from the Writing Test, along with the scores from the Spelling and Handwriting Tests, will contribute to your child's overall level for Writing (see page 47).

An example story is marked on pages 36–8.

Note to parent

You may notice that your child's level for "style" is different from his or her level for "organisation" or "punctuation". It is possible to achieve different levels for these different categories.

The marking keys show what is needed to achieve each level. By analysing your child's writing in such detail, you will be able to see what he or she does well and where the writing needs to develop. When your child is planning other writing, discuss how he or she could take account of particular features from the marking key. For example, if you notice that the events are disjointed and do not relate well in the story your child wrote for this test, you might discuss how the events could link together sensibly when your child plans another story.

Writing Answers

MARKING KEY: STORIES

How is the story written and organised?	Yes	No

JUST BELOW LEVEL 3

Does the writing include details about two or more events (real or imagined)? ☐ ☐
Does the story have more than one character? ☐ ☐
Does it have the basic elements of a story (an opening and some events)? ☐ ☐
Does it rely on simple story words (e.g. *one day... suddenly... the end*) to show it is a story? ☐ ☐
Award 6 marks if this level best describes your child's written organisation.

LEVEL 3

Does the story relate to the title? ☐ ☐
Are there some interesting details (suspense, humour, description)? ☐ ☐
Are the settings or the thoughts or feelings of the characters described? ☐ ☐
Are there several connected events that follow each other? ☐ ☐
Does the story feel as though it has been written with a reader in mind? ☐ ☐
Does the story have a simple ending? ☐ ☐
Award 12 marks if this level best describes your child's written organisation.

LEVEL 4

Does the story have a suitable opening? ☐ ☐
Does the story have a clear beginning, middle and end? ☐ ☐
Are the events of the story sensibly related with a reader in mind? ☐ ☐
Do the characters make a contribution to the story? ☐ ☐
Is there significant interaction between the characters? ☐ ☐
Is there some development of the characters, through what they say or do? ☐ ☐
Does the ending relate convincingly to the main events (e.g. not just "we all went home")? ☐ ☐
Award 15 marks if this level best describes your child's written organisation.

LEVEL 5

Is the writing well organised and well paced overall? ☐ ☐
Are there any interesting story devices, for example:
- does it start with dialogue? ☐ ☐
- does it start in the middle of a dramatic event? ☐ ☐
- does it move between times and places? ☐ ☐
- does it include a sub-plot? ☐ ☐
- does it end with a twist in the story? ☐ ☐
Is the reader's interest engaged and sustained? ☐ ☐
Are events, dialogue and description skilfully interwoven? ☐ ☐
Does the writer express a personal point of view, for example by:
- commenting on characters and events? ☐ ☐
- giving an idea of characters' thoughts and feelings? ☐ ☐
Is there some use of paragraphs to mark the beginning, main events and end? ☐ ☐
Does the ending relate convincingly to the central plot? ☐ ☐
Is it a convincing story type (e.g. mystery, true-life, myth)? ☐ ☐
Award 18 marks if this level best describes your child's written organisation.

HIGH LEVEL 5

Does the story show development of a theme (controlling idea) as well as a plot? ☐ ☐
Is it written convincingly, in appropriate paragraphs, and with confidence? ☐ ☐
Does it fully engage and sustain the reader's interest? ☐ ☐
Does it include relationships or conflict between the characters? ☐ ☐
Award 21 marks if this level best describes your child's written organisation.

Writing Answers

What style of writing is used?	Yes	No

JUST BELOW LEVEL 3

Are many of the ideas linked by "and" or "and so" or "and then"? ☐ ☐
Is simple vocabulary used (e.g. "make", "get", "thing")? ☐ ☐
Award 2 marks if this level best describes your child's writing style.

LEVEL 3

Are descriptive phrases used (e.g. "a sunny day")? ☐ ☐
Are joining words such as "but" or "because" used? ☐ ☐
Are adverbs used (e.g. "quickly", "slowly")? ☐ ☐
Award 4 marks if this level best describes your child's writing style.

LEVEL 4

Is the vocabulary interesting and lively? ☐ ☐
Are complex sentences used (e.g. phrases joined by "so that", "although", "if")? ☐ ☐
Are descriptive phrases used (e.g. "as fast as his legs could carry him")? ☐ ☐
Overall, is the writing interesting with most tenses used consistently? ☐ ☐
Award 5 marks if this level best describes your child's writing style.

LEVEL 5

Is the language vivid and interesting and does it give the intended meaning? ☐ ☐
Is there a mixture of simple and complex sentences? ☐ ☐
Is standard English used (or colloquialism and dialect for effect)? ☐ ☐
Award 6 marks if this level best describes your child's writing style.

HIGH LEVEL 5

Is the style completely appropriate and effective? ☐ ☐
Is there a suitable range of vocabulary and sentence length? ☐ ☐
Is alliteration used (e.g. "a lone laser beam lashed the side of the ship")? ☐ ☐
Is imagery used (e.g. "city lights twinkled and danced below them")? ☐ ☐
Award 7 marks if this level best describes your child's writing style.

How is punctuation used?	Yes	No

JUST BELOW LEVEL 3

Are capital letters and full stops used correctly in some places? ☐ ☐
Award 2 marks if this level best describes your child's punctuation.

LEVEL 3

Are capital letters and full stops used correctly in half the sentences? ☐ ☐
Award 4 marks if this level best describes your child's punctuation.

LEVEL 4

Are capital letters, full stops and question marks used correctly in most cases? ☐ ☐
Is there punctuation within sentences (e.g. commas, speech marks, apostrophes)? ☐ ☐
Award 5 marks if this level best describes your child's punctuation.

LEVEL 5

Are capital letters, full stops and question marks used correctly in almost all cases? ☐ ☐
Is punctuation within sentences used correctly in most cases? ☐ ☐
Award 6 marks if this level best describes your child's punctuation.

HIGH LEVEL 5

Is all punctuation very accurate? ☐ ☐
Is a wide range of punctuation used? ☐ ☐
Does punctuation help to vary the pace of the writing (i.e. are sentences varied in length)? ☐ ☐
Award 7 marks if this level best describes your child's punctuation.

Writing Answers

MARKING KEY: INFORMATION WRITING

How is the letter written and organised?	Yes	No

JUST BELOW LEVEL 3

Does the writing contain a series of statements? ☐ ☐

Is there some sign of attempts to organise the writing (e.g. an opening, a concluding statement)? ☐ ☐

Are the points made either very brief or over-long? ☐ ☐

Award 6 marks if this level best describes your child's written organisation.

LEVEL 3

Does the writing have a simple introduction? ☐ ☐

Does the writing include a number of linked statements? ☐ ☐

Is the writing related to the topic? ☐ ☐

Does the writing contain information described in some detail to add interest? ☐ ☐

Does the writing have a simple ending? ☐ ☐

Award 12 marks if this level best describes your child's written organisation.

LEVEL 4

Does the writing have a suitable introduction or opening? ☐ ☐

Is the information presented in a way that a reader can follow? ☐ ☐

Are suitable formats used (e.g. "Dear…" for a letter)? ☐ ☐

Are the main points/aspects of information covered? ☐ ☐

Is there a reasonable amount of detail? ☐ ☐

Is there a suitable final sentence? ☐ ☐

Overall, is the writing interesting? ☐ ☐

Award 15 marks if this level best describes your child's written organisation.

LEVEL 5

Is the writing well organised and well paced overall? ☐ ☐

Does the opening make clear the purpose of the writing? ☐ ☐

Is the reader's interest engaged and sustained? ☐ ☐

Is the level of formality generally appropriate? ☐ ☐

Are the main issues covered? ☐ ☐

Are individual points adequately covered? ☐ ☐

Are individual points sensibly organised and linked? ☐ ☐

Award 18 marks if this level best describes your child's written organisation.

HIGH LEVEL 5

Is the piece really well written? ☐ ☐

Are points relevant and well organised? ☐ ☐

Is the level of detail appropriate and balanced? ☐ ☐

Is there a strong introduction and conclusion? ☐ ☐

Does the writer express his or her views with authority? ☐ ☐

Are ideas organised into paragraphs to mark introduction, middle and conclusion? ☐ ☐

Award 21 marks if this level best describes your child's written organisation.

Writing
Answers

What style of writing is used?		Yes	No

JUST BELOW LEVEL 3

Are sentences simple, like speech (e.g. many sentences starting "there is")? ☐ ☐
Are many sentences linked by "and" or "then" or "but"? ☐ ☐
Is vocabulary simple (e.g. "make", "get", "do")? ☐ ☐
Award 2 marks if this level best describes your child's writing style.

LEVEL 3

Does it show an awareness of the intended reader by using appropriate vocabulary? ☐ ☐
Are descriptive phrases used (e.g. "a well behaved child, "a sunny day")? ☐ ☐
Are joining words such as "but" or "because" used? ☐ ☐
Are adverbs used (e.g. "quickly", "slowly")? ☐ ☐
Award 4 marks if this level best describes your child's writing style.

LEVEL 4

Is the vocabulary precise and varied (with suitable technical words used)? ☐ ☐
Are complex sentences used (e.g. phrases joined by "so that", although", "if")? ☐ ☐
Are phrases used to clarify meaning (e.g. "with an emblem on top")? ☐ ☐
Award 5 marks if this level best describes your child's writing style.

LEVEL 5

Is the language precise, using technical and specific words where needed? ☐ ☐
Is there a mixture of simple and complex sentences? ☐ ☐
Award 6 marks if this level best describes your child's writing style.

HIGH LEVEL 5

Is the style completely appropriate and effective including the level of formality? ☐ ☐
Is there a subtle variety of vocabulary and sentence lengths? ☐ ☐
Is word order changed for effect (e.g. "these objects whirling in the night sky were seen by a few" *instead of* "a few saw the objects whirling in the night sky")? ☐ ☐
Award 7 marks if this level best describes your child's writing style.

How is punctuation used?		Yes	No

JUST BELOW LEVEL 3

Is there some use of capital letters and full stops? ☐ ☐
Award 2 marks if this level best describes your child's punctuation.

LEVEL 3

Are capital letters and full stops used correctly in half the sentences? ☐ ☐
Award 4 marks if this level best describes your child's punctuation.

LEVEL 4

Are capital letters, full stops and question marks used correctly in most cases? ☐ ☐
Is there punctuation within sentences (e.g. commas, speech marks, apostrophes)? ☐ ☐
Award 5 marks if this level best describes your child's punctuation.

LEVEL 5

Are capital letters, full stops and question marks used correctly in almost all cases? ☐ ☐
Is punctuation within sentences used correctly in most cases? ☐ ☐
Award 6 marks if this level best describes your child's punctuation.

HIGH LEVEL 5

Is all punctuation very accurate? ☐ ☐
Is a wide range of punctuation used? ☐ ☐
Does punctuation help to vary the pace of the writing (i.e. are sentences or phrases of varied length)? ☐ ☐
Award 7 marks if this level best describes your child's punctuation.

USING THE MARKING KEY: AN EXAMPLE

Anna chose to write a story based on starting point 1:

②   Oh no!

It's the 20th of December and the last day of the winter term. We (me and my friend, Stacy) are walking home.

Finally we reach my front door and I wave goodbye to Stacy as she goes off to her own house. I take out my key and am about to put it in the lock when the door opens. My mum is standing there, an angry exp-ression on her face " M ... Mum!" I exclaimed in surprise "What's the matter?"

" This! Charlotte Mary Lewis is 'what's the matter '" she said. I knew that it was me that she was cross with, because she never uses my full name unless she's really mad with me ....

~~(Sometime later)~~ My mum stepped backwards into the hall and I saw my younger brother Andrew playing with a .... dog.

(Sometime ~~later~~ later)

" I'm really sorry mum I don't know how he ~~got in~~ can have got in I really don't!"

"Oh yes? then how do you know its a he? I've told you far too

many times already charlie ... you can
not have a pet, now get outside and
take that ... that ... THING with you!"
"But mum! ... where shall I go?"
"Just go for a walk and then
maybe some of that fresh air
can knock some sense into you!"
Suddenly a jet black cat ran
across my path. Before I realized
it Ruffles (as I had named the dog)
was running like the wind after
the cat. I called out after Ruffles and
even ran after him for a bit but
after a while I didn't see the point
any more and anyway I
couldn't even see him. Suddenly

there was a screech of brakes
and I rushed to the scene of the
accident ....

   Soon after Ruffles funeral it was
christmas eve and I had almost forg-
-otten about the accident in the excitment,
and any way who knows? I might get
lucky for christmas, but I know that
there will only ever be one like Ruffles...

HOW IS THE STORY WRITTEN AND ORGANISED?

Anna's story starts well, with an opening that sets the scene and establishes who the writer is pretending to be. There is a clear distinction between the beginning and central events of the story, but the ending is rushed and unclear. The switch from present to past tense in unintentional. The main characters (the girl and her mother) are essential to the plot and comment on their relationship ("she never uses my full name unless she's really mad with me") makes the writing lively. The organisation of the story shows some features of Level 5, but the rather rushed ending and the confusion about the main events means that it is best described as Level 4 for organisation; 15 marks should be awarded.

WHAT STYLE OF WRITING IS USED?

The story is written in a familiar conversational style, as though the writer is chatting to the reader. This does not mean that this is the simple "speech-like" writing often used by children working below Level 3. There are many well written, complex sentences (e.g. "My mum is standing there, an angry expression on her face", "I take out my key and am about to put it in the lock..."). There is plenty of variety in the vocabulary ("a screech of brakes") and descriptive phrases (e.g. "Ruffles... was running like the wind"). Much of the story, particularly the dialogue, is colloquial (e.g. "knock some sense into you"). Paragraphing is correct and is done very effectively. The vivid, lively style is appropriate to the type of story and makes this story easy to read. The style is best described as Level 5; 6 marks should be awarded.

HOW IS PUNCTUATION USED?

Capital letters, full stops and question marks are used correctly in most cases. Speech marks are used but accompanying commas are not always in place. Apostrophes and commas within sentences are generally used correctly. The punctuation is best described as Level 4, so 5 marks should be awarded.

HELPING ANNA TO DEVELOP HER WRITING

Overall, Anna scores 26 marks (Level 4) for her writing test. She was given a higher mark for *style*, which shows she is already developing writing skills associated with Level 5. The areas where she needs help are *organisation* and *punctuation*.

Anna's story was well organised until she reached the last paragraph. In future, when Anna is planning her writing, it would help if she could plan the ending in more detail. She should also think about what tense to use throughout the story and whether there will be a point when she wants to change the tense *for effect*. Short stories that Anna knows well could be used to show her how other writers organise the endings of their stories.

It would also help to show Anna how speech is punctuated in the stories that she is reading. When Anna finishes writing a story, she should be encouraged to read it through and check the punctuation. This would give her the opportunity to check that she has punctuated speech correctly.

PARENT'S GUIDE TO THE SPELLING TEST

Your child's version of the Spelling Test is printed on pages 18–19. Your child has to write down the missing words in his or her version as you read the story aloud. The full text of the story is printed below and you may detach this page. The words printed in **bold italics** are the words your child will have to spell.

Go through the instructions on page 18 together. Read the story through the first time without stopping. Then read it a second time, pausing in the appropriate places to allow your child to write down the missing words in his or her version.

STORY TO READ ALOUD

U.F.O.s??

Jenny and her brother Paul had heard stories about U.F.O.s landing in the field next to their house. During the summer holidays they set their alarm clocks so that they could wake up in the middle of the night…

One night, as they **looked** out of the window everything was **still** but something seemed **different**. The **silence** was quite strange: it felt as though something **would** happen at any **moment**.

The children listened carefully, **concentrating** on any new sound. At last they **heard** a humming sound which seemed to be coming **closer**. Paul gave a loud **sneeze** and the earth **shook** – or that is how it seemed! A second later, a **bright** light appeared and a huge spaceship seemed to **float** to the ground.

The children **crept** closer to the window and watched as the door of the spaceship opened. Through the door came the **tallest** people they had ever seen. The **visitors** were wearing the most **beautiful** uniforms, covered in **gold**…

Paul gave a loud snore and then **stretched**. Jenny was **sprawled** across her bed in a deep sleep. Did a U.F.O. land last night or was it all a dream?

HOW TO MARK THE SPELLING TEST

After the test, total up the number of words your child has spelled correctly. This total for the Spelling Test is converted into marks which contribute to the overall level for Writing. Enter the marks from this test on the Marking Grid on page 48. Marks should be given as follows:

Number of correct words	Marks	Number of correct words	Marks
1–2	1	11–12	6
3–4	2	13–14	7
5–6	3	15–16	8
7–8	4	17–18	9
9–10	5	19–20	10

IMPROVING YOUR CHILD'S SPELLING AT KEY STAGE 2

During Key Stage 2, your child should develop his or her skills in spelling. Spelling is best learnt when both phonic strategies (sound) and visual strategies (recognising groups of letters) are used.

In the early stages of learning to spell, children should learn to memorise short common words, e.g. *get*, *went*. Then they should learn to match sounds to letters – this should help them to spell simple words.

As your child becomes more aware of the relationship between sounds and letters, you should help him or her to see that patterns exist. These include:
- the effect of doubling the vowel, e.g. "ee" as in *sheep*, *sleep*, *freeze*
- how certain vowels and consonants combine, e.g. "ar" as in *car*, *card*, *hard*
- how some consonants combine to make particular sounds, e.g. "ch" as in *chain*, *choice*, *chase*
- how a silent "e" affects a vowel, e.g. *hop/hope*, *bit/bite*, *car/care*
- how two vowels combine to give a particular sound, e.g. "oi" as in *oil*, *boil*, *toil*
- how the grouping of two or more letters gives a particular sound, e.g. "igh" as in *sigh*, *high*, *slight*

Your child should also develop a visual sense of how words "look" and consider letter sequences in more complex words. Your child needs to get used to considering whether a word "looks right".

A useful way to help your child to memorise a spelling is to use the routine of "Look, Cover, Write, Check":

Look Look at a word and identify phonic patterns or sequences of letters within the word.

Cover Cover the word, but try to memorise the spelling.

Write Write the spelling down.

Check Check whether the written word is spelled correctly, identify any mistakes, and then try again.

Handwriting Answers

HOW TO MARK THE HANDWRITING TEST

When your child has completed the Handwriting Test, consider the questions below to decide which mark should be awarded. Sometimes you will not be able to answer "yes" to all the questions in a particular section, but overall you should feel that one set of questions comes closest to describing your child's handwriting. Enter the number of marks for this test on the Marking Grid on page 48. Then turn to page 47 to determine your child's overall levels in Writing, and in English.

Handwriting style	Yes	No	Marks
Can you read the handwriting? Is the size and shape of some letters irregular? Is the spacing between letters and words irregular?	☐ ☐ ☐	☐ ☐ ☐	1 mark
Are most letters formed correctly? Are most letters of similar size (such as h, k, l and g, y, p) the *right* size? Is the spacing between most letters and words regular?	☐ ☐ ☐	☐ ☐ ☐	2 marks
Are letters the right size most of the time? Are some letters and words written in a joined style? Is the spacing between letters and words appropriate?	☐ ☐ ☐	☐ ☐ ☐	3 marks
Are the letters the right size all of the time? Is all the handwriting joined? Can the joined handwriting be read? Is the handwriting joined correctly? Is the spacing between letters and words even?	☐ ☐ ☐ ☐ ☐	☐ ☐ ☐ ☐ ☐	4 marks
Is the writing joined and legible throughout the whole writing test? Is the joined handwriting fluent (e.g. do the letter joins seem to "flow" evenly)? Is the writing completed in a style that is consistent and confident?	☐ ☐ ☐	☐ ☐ ☐	5 marks

A sample Handwriting Test is marked on page 42.

USING THE MARKING KEY: AN EXAMPLE

> ### Take Off
>
> "All aboard!" Shouted the Spacship captain. Once the crew wore at their Stations they prepared for take off very quickly. "Three, two, one, zero", the Captain counted. Slowly, the Spacecraft rose from the ground and drifted up into the Sky. It Slipped away into the darkness just as the children were waking up.

MARKING REBECCA'S HANDWRITING

Rebecca has made a number of spelling mistakes as she copied out the handwriting passage, but this does not affect her mark for handwriting. If your child has made spelling mistakes in this test, you should award marks for handwriting style only. After you have awarded the appropriate marks for the handwriting test, discuss the spelling mistakes separately.

Rebecca's handwriting is joined and easy to read, and the spacing between words is mainly even. There are a number of instances, however, where Rebecca's letters are not the correct size. For example, in "slipped", the letter "l" is taller than the capital "I" in "It". The letter "s" is generally too large and in "drifted", the "f" is too small above the line. For this reason, Rebecca should be awarded 3 marks, since 4 marks requires correct letter size throughout the test.

With a little guided practice focusing on correct letter sizes, Rebecca would soon achieve a higher score since she is developing a confident style.

HOW TO MARK THE LEVEL 6 TEST

To mark this test, you will need to make judgements about the *quality* of your child's answers. This means that answers will not simply be "correct" or "incorrect" but you will be awarding marks on the basis of your child's ability to interpret the texts.

1   Give **1** mark if your child understands the main idea, that Eric Donnelly is no longer as *ordinary* as he claims.

Award a **second** mark if your child expands his or her answer, for example, by describing that Eric has become a personality and is "larger than life", surrounded by his possessions and exotic pets.   *2 marks*

2   Award **1** mark if your child recognises the main idea: that Eric's story should be doubted, or that there is more to the story than is initially being told in the newspaper report.

Award **2** marks if your child recognises that it is the *repetition* which suggests Eric's story should be doubted.   *2 marks*

3   Award **1** mark if your child comments that the narrator is surprised that people want these old-fashioned baths.

Give a **second** mark if your child expands his or her answer to include comments such as "it is only people who did not have to grow up with these baths, as Eric and the narrator did, that would want to buy them."

Award a **third** mark if your child identifies the suggestion that only rich people are buying the baths.   *3 marks*

4   The main idea here is for your child to explain why the examples he or she has chosen are amusing.

Give **1** mark for a single example, e.g. "the writer calls Eric's dog a wolf" or "the other children were funny – one wanted to keep a tooth in a box".

Give **2** marks for an example where there is a direct reference to the text, e.g. "Eric owns a samoyed which the narrator calls 'a kind of very fluffy wolf'".

Give **3** marks where more than *one* example is given and there is at least one direct reference to the text, e.g.: "Eric owns a samoyed which the narrator calls 'a kind of very fluffy wolf'. Eric calls himself 'a kind of rag-and-bone man' with the kind of confidence of a tycoon who isn't one any more."   *3 marks*

5   Give **1** mark for identifying that Anita Roddick was irritated with the major cosmetic companies.

Award **2** marks if the answer makes reference to at least *two* of the following reasons for her irritation:
- she couldn't buy small sizes
- she was too intimidated to exchange unsatisfactory products that she didn't like
- she was paying a lot for "fancy packaging" which she didn't want   *2 marks*

6   **a**   Give **1** mark total if *three* of the following actions are mentioned:
- she sprayed strawberry essence on the pavement
- she put out old-fashioned sandwich boards
- she got local art students to make posters
- she drenched the front of the shop with exotic perfume oils
- she hung branches of dried flowers from the ceiling
- she put out pot-pourri

43

- she never stayed behind the counter
- she spoke directly to her customers about her products

Award a **second** mark where at least three of the above actions are mentioned *and* there is an explanation as to why at least one of the actions was unusual, e.g. "It is very unusual for people to go round spraying the streets with strawberry essence but Anita did this so that the pathway to her shop smelled exotic."

Award a **third** mark where three actions are mentioned *and all three* have an explanation as to why the action would be considered unusual.   *3 marks*

b Give **1** mark for an answer identifying that Anita Roddick attracted a lot of different people to The Body Shop, e.g. students, young mothers, day trippers, foreign visitors and even men.

Give **2** marks where a reason is given for a particular group finding the shop attractive, e.g. "older women liked re-usable bottles, and the shop was classless".   *2 marks*

7 Anita Roddick travels for five months every year to look for new products, to trade and to talk to different women to find out what they use on their skin and hair in order to groom themselves.   *1 mark*

8 Give **1** mark for an answer identifying that she feels that you can learn more about people if you share ideas with them.

Award **1** mark for identifying that Anita believes sharing can provide opportunities for people to help themselves.   *2 marks*

9 Your child should explain his or her preference:

Give **1** mark for a single reason, e.g. "I liked the way Anita Roddick's approach to business includes an awareness of environmental issues".

Give **2** marks where a reason is given *and* direct reference is made to the text, e.g. "I prefer Anita's approach because I think her approach to recycling materials is good for the earth" *or* "I think Eric showed lots of clever ways of making money – he even had ideas for making money when he was still at school by buying other children's teeth".

Give **3** marks where *two* or more reasons are given and there are at least *two* direct references to the text, e.g.: "I prefer Anita's approach because I think her approach to recycling materials is good for the Earth. Anita had a more sensible approach to business because she let her customers sample her products and she learns from what people have to tell her. Eric only had a few good ideas which seemed to involve tricking people."   *3 marks*

10 Accept "world travel" (but not for fun), "the environment", "conservation".

Do not accept "world peace".

Award 1 mark if two or more interests are correctly identified.   *1 mark*

Questions 1–10 Total: 24 marks

11 This question required your child to do some extended writing. Use the marking key on pages 45–6 to mark this question in the same way as you marked your child's Levels 3–5 Writing Test. Enter your child's marks for organisation, for grammar and punctuation, and for spelling and handwriting on the Marking Grid on page 48.   *24 marks*

Question 11 Total: 24 marks

Level 6
Answers

MARKING KEY: LEVEL 6

How is the writing organised?	Yes	No
BELOW LEVEL 6		
Is the piece really well written?	☐	☐
Are points relevant and well organised?	☐	☐
Is the level of detail appropriate and balanced?	☐	☐
Is there a strong introduction and conclusion?	☐	☐
Are ideas developed in an interesting way?	☐	☐
Are ideas or views expressed with authority?	☐	☐
Are ideas appropriately organised into paragraphs?	☐	☐
Is some information from the original texts used to support ideas and views?	☐	☐
Award 6 marks if this level best describes your child's written organisation.		

	Yes	No
LEVEL 6		
Is the piece really well written?	☐	☐
Are points relevant and well organised?	☐	☐
Is the level of detail appropriate and balanced *and* does it sustain the interest of the reader?	☐	☐
Are devices used which show an awareness of the reader (e.g. by establishing the role of the writer as a journalist)?	☐	☐
Are the main issues covered well with information from one of the texts being used?	☐	☐
Are some of the ideas and structures from the original text used?	☐	☐
Are ideas organised appropriately into paragraphs?	☐	☐
Does the final paragraph conclude with an appropriate summary which is either factual or persuasive?	☐	☐
Is the writing controlled and confident?	☐	☐
Award 12 marks if this level best describes your child's written organisation.		

How are grammar and punctuation used?	Yes	No
BELOW LEVEL 6		
Is all punctuation very accurate?	☐	☐
Is a wide range of punctuation used?	☐	☐
Does punctuation help to vary the pace of the writing (i.e. are sentences and phrases of varied length)?	☐	☐
Is the style completely appropriate and effective, including the level of formality?	☐	☐
Is there a subtle variety of vocabulary and sentence lengths?	☐	☐
Is word order changed for effect?	☐	☐
Are appropriate choices made between standard English and slang?	☐	☐
Award 3 marks if this level best describes your child's grammar and punctuation.		

	Yes	No
LEVEL 6		
Is a wide range of punctuation used?	☐	☐
Does the punctuation vary the pace of the writing and clarify meaning?	☐	☐
Are commas used to show divisions between clauses?	☐	☐
Are commas used to clarify meaning?	☐	☐
Are colons, semi-colons or dashes used to clarify meaning?	☐	☐
Is the style of writing appropriate for a published article?	☐	☐
Is there an appropriate and sustained level of formality in the writing?	☐	☐
Is there a mixture of short and long sentences that are used effectively?	☐	☐
Is there variety in vocabulary used (e.g. a varied use of verbs and adjectives)?	☐	☐
Award 6 marks if this level best describes your child's grammar and punctuation.		

How are spelling and handwriting used to present the writing?	Yes	No

BELOW LEVEL 6

Is handwriting joined, fluent and easy to read? ☐ ☐

Are words with regular complex patterns spelled correctly (e.g. "satisfied", "appearance", "apprehensive")? ☐ ☐

Award 3 marks if this level best describes your child's spelling and handwriting.

LEVEL 6

Is handwriting joined, fluent and legible? ☐ ☐

Is the writing style altered appropriately if the article requires any special features (e.g. sub-headings)? ☐ ☐

Is spelling accurate, including the spelling of irregular words (e.g. "guarantee", "nuisance")? ☐ ☐

Award 6 marks if this level best describes your child's spelling and handwriting.

Determining your child's level

FINDING YOUR CHILD'S LEVEL IN READING AND WRITING

When you have marked your child's Reading Test, enter the marks scored for each section of the test on the Marking Grid overleaf. Then add them up.

Using this total for the Reading Test, look at the chart below to determine your child's level for Reading:

Reading

Below Level 3	Level 3	Level 4	Level 5	High Level 5
up to 15	16–25	26–35	36–45	46+

When you have marked your child's Writing, Spelling and Handwriting Tests, enter the marks scored for each section on the Marking Grid overleaf. Then add them up. Using this total for all three tests, look at the chart below to determine your child's overall level for Writing.

Writing (including Spelling and Handwriting)

Below Level 3	Level 3	Level 4	Level 5	High Level 5
up to 25	26–33	34–41	42–49	50

FINDING YOUR CHILD'S OVERALL LEVEL IN ENGLISH

After you have worked out separate levels for Reading and Writing, add up your child's total marks. Use this total and the chart below to determine your child's overall level in English. The chart also shows you how your child's level in these tests compares with the target level for his or her age group.

Total for Reading and Writing

Below Level 3	Level 3	Level 4	Level 5	High Level 5
up to 41	42–59	60–77	78–95	96+
Working towards target level for age group		Working at target level	Working beyond target level	

In the Key Stage 2 English Test, Level 6 will not be awarded if Level 5 has not been achieved on the main tests for Reading, Writing and Spelling and Handwriting. If your child achieved a Level 5 in *both* Reading and Writing above, you may wish to set the Level 6 Test. Enter the marks scored for each section of the test on the Marking Grid overleaf. Then add them up. The chart below shows whether or not your child is working at Level 6.

Level 6 Test

Below Level 6	Level 6
up to 36	37+

Marking Grid

Reading   Pages 1–13

Section	Marks available	Marks scored
Amazing U.F.O.s	19	
The Disastrous Dog	31	
Total	**50**	

Writing   Pages 14–20

Section	Marks available	Marks scored
How is the story/letter written and organised?	21	
What style of writing is used?	7	
How is punctuation used?	7	
Spelling marks (see page 39)	**10**	
Handwriting marks (see page 41)	**5**	
Total	**50**	

Level 6   Pages 21–26

Section	Marks available	Marks scored
Test questions 1–10	24	
Question 11: how is the writing organised?	12	
Question 11: how are grammar and punctuation used?	6	
Question 11: how are spelling and punctuation used to present the writing?	6	
Total	**48**	

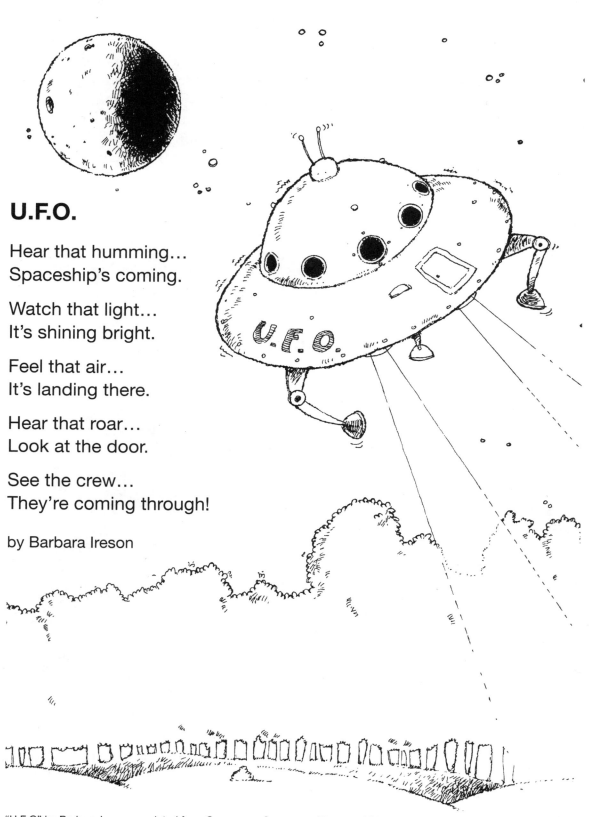

U.F.O.

Hear that humming…
Spaceship's coming.

Watch that light…
It's shining bright.

Feel that air…
It's landing there.

Hear that roar…
Look at the door.

See the crew…
They're coming through!

by Barbara Ireson

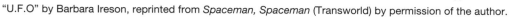

"U.F.O" by Barbara Ireson, reprinted from *Spaceman, Spaceman* (Transworld) by permission of the author.

Target Earth

1952 was a particularly good year for U.F.O. sightings. As well as the "Washington Invasion", described below, there were some 1500 reports of U.F.O.s that year in different parts of the world and more than 300 of them remain unexplained.

U.F.O.s often occur in waves like this. Sometimes U.F.O. activity is confined to particular regions, where people who have never heard of U.F.O.s report an unusual number over a short period. Time of year also seems to play a part in the sightings – U.F.O.s are particularly active in spring and there is a summer season in July.

Of course, newspaper reports contribute to the upsurge of U.F.O. incidents.

Once the idea of U.F.O.s has been planted in people's minds they are more likely to start "meeting Martians" and their "sightings" have to be treated with caution.

The Washington Invasion

Place: Washington, USA
Date: July 19 and 26, 1952
Time: From 10:00 p.m.

One of the most famous of all U.F.O. events is the so-called "Washington Invasion". One summer evening the citizens of the United States' capital were treated to a display by five strange lights which manoeuvred for hours over the White House, the city and the countryside around.

A week later, the lights reappeared. This time there were between 6 and 12 of them and they moved too fast to be aircraft.

Two F94 jet interceptors were scrambled to investigate them, but the pilots could find nothing and returned to base. However, when a third jet was sent up the pilot radioed that he was approaching a

cluster of huge blue and white lights. As he closed in on them the lights moved to form a ring around him and travelled along with him for about 15 seconds before moving slowly away.

The Flying Cross

Place: Hatherleigh, Devon, England
Date: October 24, 1967
Time: 4:00 a.m.

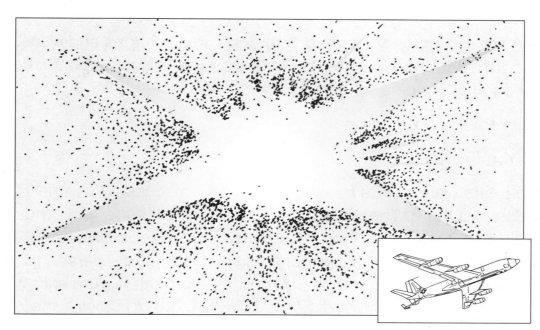

Police constables Roger Willey and Clifford Waycott were on routine night duty in their patrol car when they suddenly saw bright lights in the shape of a large cross pulsating in the sky ahead of them. As the patrol car drove towards it, the cross moved silently away. The policemen chased through the narrow lanes after it, but the cross always managed to accelerate away from them. Eventually it moved off across the fields and the policemen gave up.

Once the sighting found its way into the papers, flying crosses were reported up and down the country.

For a time it was thought the lighted "cross" might be a tanker plane, like the one shown in the small picture above, surrounded by other, smaller aircraft. The Ministry of Defence agreed that refuelling was taking place in that area, but said that it had been completed by 9:00 p.m., several hours before the flying cross sightings. Another suggestion was that the policemen had chased the planet Venus, which was unusually bright in the sky at that time. This seems unlikely, however, and the flying cross mystery has never been solved.

Strange Tales

The Disastrous Dog

by Penelope Lively

This is the story of what happened to Mr and Mrs Roper, and their nine-year-old son Paul when they went to the local Animal Sanctuary to choose a dog.

The Animal Sanctuary seethed with dogs, in all shapes and sizes. They rushed around in wire netting enclosures, all barking at once, tail-wagging, jumping up and down.

"Oy...!" Paul looked around.

"Oy! You there..."

His parents were on the far side of the yard, discussing a terrier. The Warden had gone. The voice came from none of them. And I must explain that it was, and Paul immediately understood this, no ordinary voice. It was, as it were, a voice in the head – person to person, invisible, like a telephone. But the words that were said were ordinary and straightforward. Standard English. And so was the tone, which was distinctly bossy.

He looked at the dogs, carefully. They were all dashing around except for one, a nondescript brown animal with a stumpy tail and one white ear, which stood squarely beside the fence staring at Paul.

Paul glanced over at his parents; they were not looking in his direction. He stared back at the brown dog. "Did you say something?" he asked, feeling foolish.

"Too right I did," said the dog. "Do you live in a house or a flat?"

"A house. In the country."

"Central heating? Garden?"

"Yes. Listen, how come you..."

The dog interrupted. "Sounds a reasonable billet. Get your parents over here and I'll do my stuff. Homeless dog act. Never fails."

"Can they all?" asked Paul, waving at the other dogs. "Talk?"

The dog spluttered contemptuously. "'Course not. Ordinary mob, that's all they are."

There was something not altogether attractive about the dog's personality, but Paul could not help being intrigued. "Then how did you learn?"

"Because I know what's what," snapped the dog.

"And why me? Why don't you talk to my dad?"

"Unfortunately," said the dog, "the adult of the species tends to have what you might call a closed mind. I've tried, believe you me. No go. It's only you small fry that are at all receptive. More's the pity. Go on – tell your mum and dad to come over and have a look at me."

Paul wasn't entirely pleased at being called small fry. He hesitated. The dog came closer to the fence and stared up at him, with slightly narrowed eyes. "Think about it," he said.

"We just want a dog that can bark," said Paul.

The dog flung back his head and let out a volley of ear-splitting barks. "That do?"

Mr and Mrs Roper, abandoning the terrier, had come across. The dog immediately hurled himself at the wire fence with a devastating display of tail-wagging, grinning and licking. When Mrs Roper

stooped to pat him he rolled over on his back with his eyes shut and squirmed in apparent ecstasy. Mrs Roper said, "Oh, isn't he sweet!" The dog, briefly, opened one eye. He then got up and squatted in front of Mr Roper in an attitude of abject obedience. Finally, he rushed off as though in pursuit of an unseen enemy and did some more barking, of hideous ferocity and quite deafening.

Well, I don't need to tell you what happened.

To say that the dog settled in is to put it mildly: he established himself. Within a matter of days. He got his basket moved from the cloakroom by feigning illness; Mrs Roper, gazing down at him, said anxiously, "I think perhaps he's cold in here. We'd better let him sleep in the kitchen by the boiler." The dog feebly wagged his tail and staggered to his feet. The first time they took him for a walk he developed a limp after the first mile. Paul examined his paws. He said, "I can't see anything wrong."

"Shut up," snarled the dog. "I'm crippled. I'm not one for all this hearty outdoor stuff, let's get that straight from the start."

Paul had to carry him home.

On the fourth day the dog said, "Tell her I don't like that rabbit-flavoured meat she's giving me. I want the beef and oxtail flavour. And more biscuits."

"Tell her yourself," said Paul sulkily. He was getting tired of being ordered about.

"Some people," snapped the dog.

They called him Mick. It didn't seem to suit him particularly, but then it would have been hard to know what would. "What's your name?" Paul had asked, on the first day.

"Depends," said the dog. "One has run through a good many, as it happens. Suit yourselves."

So Mick it was.

His favourite activity was sleeping. Preferably after a hefty meal and on the best sofa or one of the beds. "Most dogs," said Paul, "rush about all day sniffing at things and asking to be taken for walks."

Mick yawned. "That's their problem. Me, I've learned how to keep my head down and have a comfortable life. Push off, there's a good boy, I want a kip."

To begin with, he barked at the postman and the milkman and the man who came to read the meter. On the fifth day, he slept through the window-cleaner and a man selling brushes and a lady collecting for the Red Cross. Paul said, "You're supposed to bark. That's what they got you for."

"I barked my head off all yesterday," said Mick sullenly. "Besides, there's a rate for the job. If they want more action, then what about something extra on the side? The odd chocolate biscuit. A nice chop."

Mr Roper, by now, was beginning to have doubts. He observed that Mick seemed a somewhat slothful sort of dog. Mrs Roper, always keen to see the best in people, wondered if perhaps he was a rather old dog and too much shouldn't be expected. Mick, looking worn, limped to his food bowl and stood there gazing at her soulfully.

"He is awfully greedy," said Mrs Roper. "I don't know how it's happened but he's somehow got me giving him *three* meals a day

Strange Tales

now." Paul knew only too well how it had happened.

"He's lazy," said Mr Roper. "No two ways about it, I'm afraid." He took Mick for a five-mile walk; Mick rolled in a muddy ditch and then came back and rolled on the sitting room carpet. "That'll teach 'em," he said. Paul, looking at his mother's face, realised with interest that Mick might go too far before long.

He got fatter and fatter. His attacks on the postman were more and more unconvincing. But the crunch came on the day the men came to collect the television for repair when everyone was out. They went round to the back door, which had been left unlocked, came in, removed the television and drove away in a van.

Mrs Roper, when they brought it back, apologised. "I'm afraid our dog must have been a bit of a nuisance. I'd meant to lock him up before you came."

The television man laughed. "Not him. Fast asleep, he was, and then woke up and took one look and scarpered outside. Wouldn't say boo to a goose, he wouldn't."

That did it. "He's useless," said Mr Roper. Mrs Roper, always prepared to give the benefit of the doubt, suggested that perhaps Mick knew the difference between television repair men and burglars. "Not unless he could read the writing on the side of the van," said Mr Roper grimly. "He's going back to the Animal Sanctuary, and that's that."

Paul, secretly, heaved a sigh of relief. Mick had gone too far. And now, with any luck, they could get another dog: a speechless dog-like dog. What would happen to Mick he could not imagine, but he had a fairly strong feeling that he was well able to take care of himself.

Extract from "The Disastrous Dog" by Penelope Lively adapted and reproduced from *Uninvited Ghosts and Other Stories*, William Heinemann Ltd, 1984; reprinted by permission of Reed Consumer Books.

Teeth

by Jan Mark

Eric still lives in the town where we grew up. He says he wants to stay close to his roots. That's a good one. You can say that again. Roots.

Some people are rich because they are famous. Some people are famous just for being rich. Eric Donnelly is one of the second sort, but I knew him before he was either, when we were at Victoria Road Primary together. I don't really *know* Eric any more, but I can read about him in the papers any time, same as you can. He was in one of the colour supplements last Sunday, with a photograph of his house all over a double-page spread. You need a double-page spread to take in Eric these days. He was being interviewed about the things he really considers important in life, which include, in the following order, world peace, conservation, foreign travel (to promote world peace, of course, not for *fun*), his samoyeds (a kind of very fluffy wolf) and his wife. He didn't mention money but anyone who has ever known Eric – for three years like I did or even for five minutes – knows that on Eric's list it comes at the top, way in front of world peace. In the photo he was standing with the wife and three of the samoyeds in front of the house, trying to look ordinary. To *prove* how ordinary he is he was explaining how he used to be very poor and clawed his way up using only his own initiative. Well, that's true as far as it goes: his own initiative and his own claws – and other people's teeth. He didn't mention the teeth.

"Well," says Eric modestly, in the Sunday supplement, "it's a standing joke, how I got started. Cast-iron baths." That too is true as far as it goes. When Eric was fifteen he got a job with one of those firms that specialize in house clearances. One day they cleared a warehouse which happened to contain two hundred and fifty Victorian cast-iron baths with claw feet. It occurred to Eric that there were a lot of people daft enough to actually *want* a Victorian bath with claw feet; people, that is, who hadn't had to grow up with them, so he bought the lot at a knock-down price, did them up and flogged them. That bit's well known, but in the Sunday supplement he decided to come clean. He came clean about how he'd saved enough money to buy the baths in the first place by collecting scrap metal, cast-offs, old furniture and returnable bottles. "A kind of rag-and-bone man," said Eric, with the confidence of a tycoon who can afford to admit that he used to be a rag-and-bone man because he isn't one any more. He still didn't mention the teeth.

I first met Eric Donnelly in the Odeon cinema one Saturday morning during the kids' show. I'd seen him around at school before – he was in the year above mine – but here he was sitting next to me. I was trying to work out one of my front teeth which had been loose for ages and was now hanging by a thread. I could open and shut it, like a door, but it kept getting stuck and I'd panic in case it wouldn't go right side round again. In the middle of *Thunder Riders* it finally came unstuck and shot out. I just managed to field it and after having a quick look I shoved it in my pocket. Eric leaned over and said in my earhole, "What are you going to do with that, then?"

"Put it under me pillow," I said. "Me mum'll give me sixpence for it."

"Oh, the tooth fairy," said Eric. "Give it to us, then, I'll pay you sixpence."

"Do you collect them?" I asked him.

"Sort of," said Eric. "Go on – sixpence. What about it?"

"But me mum knows it's loose," I said.

"Sevenpence, then."

"She'll want to know where it went."

"Tell her you swallowed it," Eric said. "She won't care."

He was right, and I didn't care either, although I cared a lot about the extra penny. You might not believe this, but a penny – an old penny – was worth something then, that is, you noticed the difference between having it and not having it. Eric was already holding it out on his palm in the flickering darkness – one penny and two threepenny bits. I took them and gave him the tooth in a hurry – I didn't want to miss any more of *Thunder Riders*.

"Your tooth's gone, then," my mum said, when I came home and she saw the gap.

"I swallowed it," I said, looking sad. "Never mind," she said, and I could see she was relieved that the tooth fairy hadn't got to fork out another sixpence. I'd lost two teeth the week before.

It was half-term that weekend so I didn't see Eric till we were back at school on Wednesday. Yes, Wednesday. Half-terms were short, then, like everything else: trousers, money... He was round the back of the bog with Brian Ferris.

"Listen," Eric was saying, "threepence, then."

"Nah," said Brian, "I want to keep it."

"But you said your mum didn't believe in the tooth fairy," Eric persisted. "You been losing teeth for two years for *nothing*! If you let me have it you'll get threepence – *four*pence."

"I want it," said Brian. "I want to keep it in a box and watch it go rotten."

"Fivepence," said Eric.

"It's mine. I want it." Brian walked away and Eric retired defeated, but at dinner time I caught him at it again with Mary Arnold, over by the railings.

"How much does your tooth fairy give you?" he asked.

"A shilling," said Mary, smugly.

"No deal, then," Eric said, shrugging.

"But I'll let *you* have it for thixpenth," said Mary, and smiled coyly. She always was soft, that Mary.

I started to keep an eye on Eric after that, him and his collection. It wasn't *what* he was collecting that was strange, it was the fact that he was prepared to pay. I noticed several things. First, the size of the tooth had nothing to do with the amount that Eric would cough up. Also, that he would never go above elevenpence. That was his ceiling. No one ever got a shilling out of Eric Donnelly, even for a great big thing with roots.

Now Eric, although he was a year older, was smaller than me. That day I followed him home.

It was not easy to follow Eric home. They tended to marry early in that family so Eric not only had a full set of grandparents but also two great-grandmothers and enough aunties to upset the national average. Eric was always going to stay with one of them or another. He was heading for one of his great-grandmas that evening, along Jubilee Crescent. I nailed him down by the phone box.

"Listen, Donnelly," I said. "What are you doing with all them teeth?"

Give him credit, he didn't turn a hair. A lot of kids would have got scared, but not Eric. He just said, "You got one for me, then?"

"Well, no," I said, "but I might have by Saturday."

"Sevenpence?" said Eric, remembering the previous transaction, I suppose. He had a head for figures.

"Maybe," I said, "but I want to know what you do with them."

"What if I won't tell you?" Eric said.

"I'll knock all yours out," I suggested, so he told me. As I thought, it was all down to the grannies and aunties. They were sorry for poor little Eric – Dad out of work, and no pocket money. If he lost a tooth while he was staying with one of them he put it under the pillow and the tooth fairy paid up. There being two great-grannies, two grannies and seven aunties, it was hard for anyone to keep tabs on the number of teeth Eric lost and it hadn't taken him long to work out that if he didn't overdo things he could keep his eleven tooth fairies in business for years. Kids who didn't have a tooth fairy of their own were happy to flog him a fang for a penny. If he had to pay more than sixpence the tooth went to Great-Granny Ennis, who had more potatoes than the rest of them put together.

By the time that he was eleven I calculate that Eric Donnelly had lost one hundred teeth, which is approximately twice as many as most of us manage to lose in a lifetime. With the money he saved he bought a second-hand barrow and toured the streets touting for scrap, returnable bottles and so on, which was what earned him enough to buy the two hundred and fifty Victorian baths with claw feet which is the beginning of the public part of Eric's success story, where we came in. I suppose there is some justice in the fact that at thirty-eight Eric no longer has a single tooth he can call his own.

No – I am not Eric's dentist. I am his dustman. Occasionally I turn up just as Eric is leaving for a board meeting. He flashes his dentures at me in a nervous grin and I give him a cheery wave like honest dustmen are meant to do.

"Morning, Donnelly," I shout merrily. "Bought any good teeth lately?" He hates that.

Extract from the story "Teeth" by Jan Mark, adapted and reproduced with permission from *Hundreds and Hundreds*, edited by Peter Dickenson, Puffin, 1984.

Anita Roddick

The first branch of The Body Shop opened in Brighton in 1976. Twenty years later there are almost 1500 branches in over 40 countries. The Body Shop is concerned about the environment, the testing of cosmetics on animals, and the protection of human rights around the world. The company buys the ingredients for some of its products from people who live in the rainforest. This gives these people a way to feed their families. Anita Roddick founded The Body Shop – in this passage from "Body and Soul" she describes how it all started.

Brighton shopkeepers opening up for business in the spring of 1976 occasionally had cause to sniff the air, then pause and scratch their heads at the curious sight of this odd woman in dungarees with unruly dark hair walking down the street intently spraying strawberry essence onto the pavement. It was not a madwoman – it was me, laying a scented trail to the door of The Body Shop in the hope that potential customers would follow it.

Believe me, I was prepared to try anything in those early days to get customers into my shop. I wanted to get passers-by to stop, so I put big, old-fashioned sandwich boards outside and got local art students to make posters promoting one or another of the products. I drenched the front of the shop in the most exotic perfume oils so that it always smelled wonderful as you approached; inside I hung huge branches of dried flowers from the ceiling, and there was fragrant pot-pourri everywhere.

Once I had got people inside, it was all down to me. I never *sold* anything to anyone, at least not in the way that selling was then understood; it was not my style to be a pushy saleswoman. In the retail trade, sales staff tend to use counters as a refuge to avoid making contact with customers. That was not me: I was never behind the counter. I would be tidying a shelf next to someone and I would dab something like the Glycerine and Rosewater Lotion on the back of my hand and say: "Umm, I love the smell of this. Here, try it. What do you think?"

I didn't know anything about business when I opened the first Body Shop. The vocabulary of business was part of a language I did not speak. And I certainly had no ambitions to start a big international company. I didn't want to change the world; I just wanted to survive and be able to feed my kids. The extent of my business knowledge went no further than the grim knowledge that I would have to take in £300 a week to stay open. But I did know how to trade.

I started with a kind of grace which clung to the notion that in business you didn't tell lies. I didn't think of myself as an entrepreneur. My motivation for going into the cosmetics business was irritation: I was annoyed by the fact that you couldn't buy small sizes of everyday cosmetics and angry with myself that I was always too intimidated to go back and exchange something if I didn't like it. I also recognised that a lot of the money I was paying for a product was being spent on fancy packaging which I didn't want. So I opened a small shop to sell a small range of cosmetics made from natural ingredients in five different sizes in the cheapest possible plastic containers.

If it hadn't worked, I would have found something else to do. But it did work. And I am glad. Without my entirely understanding it, and certainly without my planning it, the shop seemed to appeal to lots of different kinds of customers – to students, young mothers, day trippers, foreign visitors. Even guys liked to come in and look around. Women of my Mum's age liked the notion of returnable

bottles, perhaps because it reminded them of those thrifty days during and after the war. It was classless, friendly and stylish; people felt comfortable even if they were only browsing.

Today, The Body Shop is an international company rapidly expanding around the world and in those intervening years I have learned a lot. I spend about five months every year travelling the world looking for new products, and I make sure everyone knows where I have been, whom I have met and what ideas have surfaced, whether it is paper-making in Nepal, or finding a use for brazil nuts in the Amazon.

Accompanied by an interpreter and sometimes an anthropologist, I am happy to go anywhere in the world to look for trade and to talk to women about what they use – and what their mothers and grandmothers used – to polish and cleanse and protect their skin. What I have learned is that it is better to *share* than to give or to receive. I have learned that the poorest people are anything but helpless when given the slightest opportunity to help themselves.

I have also learned the pure joy that is to be obtained from mixing with simple people whose lives are untainted by what we have laughably described as "progress".

During the late eighties and early nineties The Body Shop has combined with Friends of the Earth, Survival International and Greenpeace to run joint campaigns on acid rain, recycling, the vanishing countryside, the ozone layer and the green consumer. Our staff achieved what no other environmental group internationally has ever achieved: in less than a month they collected more than one million signatures to protest against the burning of the rainforests. All we did was bring the issue to the marketplace and use our shops as a campaign platform. We donated window displays and provided posters and leaflets, and our staff and customers did the rest.

When people talk about The Body Shop they talk about our philosophy, our campaigning, our social and educational policies and the way we have managed to humanise business practices.

What everyone wants to know – and no one seems to be able to work out – is if there is a direct link between the company's values and its success. When people ask us how we do it I tell them it is easy.

First, you have to have fun.

Second, you have to put love where your labour is.

Third, you have to go in the opposite direction to everyone else.

I don't know how many of them understand what we are saying, but the fact is that we are still pretty lonely on our home territory. It's a great pity: personally I would go to the other end of the earth to learn from a company that was trying to make the world a better place.

This extract was adapted and reproduced with permission from the book *Body and Soul*, published by Ebury Press, with the kind permission of The Body Shop International Plc and Russell Miller, 1996. Photographs reproduced by kind permission of The Body Shop.